WINDOWS
TO THE
SOUL

A Little Book of Wisdoms

WINDOWS TO THE SOUL

A Little Book of Wisdoms

Yvonne Banks-Martin

Mystics of the World, Publisher
Longboat Key, Florida

WINDOWS TO THE SOUL
A Little Book of Wisdoms

For information contact:
Mystics of the World
Longboat Key, Florida
www.mysticsoftheworld.com

Book design by Palomar Print Design

Banks-Martin, Yvonne
Windows to the soul / Yvonne Banks-Martin

ISBN 978-1-946362-30-8
I. Mysticism –– Miscellanea. I. Title.

Introduction

The author has practiced daily meditation for the past fifty years, and during these times the Wisdoms we see here have emerged. But this has not happened by chance. There has always been a firm and constant intention to stay with three simple questions: Why I am here, what is this "I", and where does it exist?

If these questions seem like a reasonable starting point towards understanding our existence, what follows requires passion and perseverance. It requires us to develop our practice of sitting in stillness, staying with these questions as a friend in need, never once content to neglect their presence. Without knowing it, we are building the foundation for a new path. And along the way, if we stay still long enough, personal and collective belief are pared away to reveal a permanent internal state of absolute surrender, a place of readiness to receive what is given. Only then we may see.

Each Wisdom is, as the title of the book suggests, a window to the soul, the soul of the individual who is reading them. And what is meant by Soul? The soul is the individualized aspect of the Divine. It is unique, eternal, a dimension hidden beyond the mind. Unfortunately, until we discover it, it lies dormant and we remain unaware. Each Wisdom has arisen from that place, and is instantly recognized by the soul of the reader. As such, they are awakenings. Continual reading of them assist us on the journey of recognizing and inhabiting our inner state. Our reality, our perception begins to change.

It is best to receive the Wisdoms with an open mind. In many ways, nothing else is needed for them to begin their revelation. Their essence is innocent and pure. If you allow them, they will meet you. They will resonate in the state of consciousness that exists prior to thought. This is where the essence, the pure substance of you resides. This point of discovery, once sensed, gives you the opportunity to expand your reality, and to experience a deep sense of freedom. This is the birth of your soul.

The wisdoms are not intended as thoughts for the day, though they can be used in that way. More so, they encourage the spiritual practice of going beyond thought to establish what is true and what is not. This entails nothing short of internal revolution; an expansion into the unknown territory that exists within us all, that is our birthright, our home. The Wisdoms spring from this sacred ground and in turn offer that sacred ground to you. These seeds will be planted in the soil of your soul which in time may become a tree filled with spiritual fruits.

This book of wisdoms is split into five parts, each prefaced by a vignette of a transcendental moment. Transcendental moments exist beyond the boundary of the self. They are spontaneous or sometimes indeed moments when you dip into the never ending and eternal field of your soul. This generally occurs when you are not in the way, meaning there is no awareness of you operating from the conditioned material mind. In these moments your soul becomes your teacher as you give birth to her.

PART ONE

Expansion of the self into the universe

Returning home from an evening with friends, the night was unusually dark. But as I walked, the moon glided from behind cloud cover, illuminating the pathway. It was bigger and brighter than I had ever seen before. I stopped for a moment, beckoned by its intensity. As I continued to stare, I noticed my sense of self shrinking to a pinpoint of insignificance. Only then I felt the moon pulling me, and I began to expand and grow into the universe, going beyond the beyond. As I moved into the heart of the creation, I felt my existence was timeless and endless.

In the face of this ever-expanding universe, I was nothing but at the same time I knew I had been granted unlimited access to its immensity in an expanded state of being. It all resided within me. The expansion was internal and dependent on me being there; it couldn't occur without me. It existed and I was the existence of its existence. I was only fifteen years old at the time and with hindsight it was too much for my young, adolescent brain. I had been taken to the edge of what we actually are. The experience was too over-whelming. I looked away and carried on walk-ing.

But I have never forgotten that night. It has stayed with me in its wonder and immensity and I have never quite looked at the moon, myself, humanity or indeed creation, in the same way again.

Indeed, many times I have returned to visit that place on the edge. I have learned that we are immense and wonderful beings, with access to inner states of knowledge and expansion that we can't even begin to imagine. I have seen my connectedness to the universe and to all within it. I have felt the eternal growth of a benevolent universe. I have experienced myself as it and it as me.

Nothing can ever harm you,
only the thought that something can.

~~~

Your best defence is Love.

Enter into agreement with Life instead of
expecting Life to enter into agreement with you.

~~~

There is nothing to forgive.

When you come to the blank piece of paper
inside of yourself, don't write on it.

~~~

The intellect is the avenue
for the awareness of Truth.

Everything in life will meet you
at exactly where you are.

~~~

Before you can move on in your life
you must be grateful for where you are.

All is Is, Is is All.
But what and where is Is?
Is is the state that exists between the opposites.
Is is the very ground and silence of Creation.
It exists within you.

~~~

Resistance always underlies suffering.

Often the need for reason
is an excuse for action.

~~~

Destiny doesn't exist in the future; it exists now
and you can choose to change it.

To be in a state of humility
is to be in absolute balance with your
greatness, power, and magnificence.

~~~

Not acting on what you know to be the truth
is always the cause of conflict.

The ending of all that we have become is the prelude to the vision of what we actually are.

~~~

When you are totally alive there is no choice.

Never look outside of yourself for Truth.
Instead read the Universal Book of Life, which
is inside of you. Its pages and words are infinite.

~~~

To finish the process that awareness inspires,
you must act.

In Truth there are no opposites. Truth just Is.

~~

You are walking in footprints
you have already made.

We begin from the point of nothing. In
the surrender to your nothingness you are
completely free and innocent.

~~~

Do not question with your mind,
rather with your heart.

Once you make the decision to let go,
there is no sense of loss.

~~~

There is no defence in Truth. To defend it is
to bring it down to a base level and destroy it.
Never defend your Truth or communicate it
to one who is in a state of defence.

Always look for the common link between you and another, not the difference. The common link binds, the difference separates.

~~~

Discipline is a natural state;
it exists where Love is.

Every adversity you meet in life serves only to
make your flame burn brighter.

~~~

Transformation is not a stagnant state; it is
an ongoing process, accessing the individual to
higher and higher states of consciousness.

All Life wants to do is to live itself through us.
All we have to do is allow it.

~~~

You are the master of transcendence
when you realize there is nothing to transcend.

You are loved whether you know it or not,
so you may as well allow yourself to feel it.

~~~

Whenever you feel like an outsider in life,
realize that you are an insider in your own life.

Conflict is the opportunity
for the awareness of Truth.

~~~

There is nothing to become; you are already
all that you are. When you see this
you are living in Truth.

The realization that there is nothing to forgive
is the ultimate act of forgiveness.

~~~

Change is natural;
it is our resistance to it that isn't.

Life is a blessing and you are
the perfume of that blessing.
How do you want your perfume to smell?

~~~

I am not my body. This body belongs to me
but I am not my body. It is the same as
I am not my house. I wander around in it
but it is only for my use.
I am not however my house.

The death of the conscience occurs when
the individual does not face his actions.

Never judge another by your own standards.
Your standards are your personal guidelines,
not your tool or excuse for judgement of others.
They are for your personal gauge and should
not be used to gauge or judge another.

Once you let go of the drama there is
very little to deal with. End the drama.

~~~

The dream can be wonderful but reality is
better. Wake up from the dream
and set yourself free.

Self-doubt comes from a frightened heart.
Keep your heart wide open and trust yourself.

~~~

You awaken in others
the attitude you have towards them.

Love asks nothing of you but to give It.

~~~

Immortality exists in the present moment and is accessed by putting all your effort and attention towards realizing reality, which is life eternal.

Judgement of another is always based on
a personal and emotional investment in
something. This separates and divides us and
disallows true relationship.

~~~

Life and death co-exist; you cannot have one
without the other. The only reason you feel
that you die is because you live without death.
Allow your self to die daily so that
the true Self may be born.

You are the creator of your own destiny,
the blueprint for your own soul.

~~~

Our greatest teachers often take the form
of our most ardent enemies.

Your conscience is never wrong.

∿∿∿

Every person you meet gives you exactly
what you need in order for you to learn
what you need to learn.

Very few people can discard
their self-image and stand naked in the world,
but to do so is total freedom and peace.

~~~

To truly be in relationship you have to end
all the rituals of relationship.

Have no fixed idea of yourself. Ideas of yourself
serve only to imprison, frame, and limit your
experience of the Limitless. This also applies
to any idea you have on another.

~~~

I could never have arrived here
if I hadn't already left there.

Be your own pupil. You already contain
everything. If you sit within yourself long
enough, in the end you will see this.
You will see Reality.

~~~

The way you see me has little to do with me
and lots to do with you.

Better to be in the dark
than in the light and not act.

~~~

We are all storytellers. Tell your story
but don't get caught up in it.

You are a manifestation of Infinity.
All that Is, is within you and available for you
to access at any given moment.

~~~

When you let go of resistance to resistance
then you are in a state of surrender.

You are the guru. You are the pupil.
You house all the questions and all the answers.

~~~

Emotions are neither positive nor negative;
it's your reaction to them that is.

It would seem that many of life's personal
problems occur because we neither know that
we are loved or, more importantly,
feel that we are loved. If you love someone,
then let them know ceaselessly,
because they may one day feel the truth
of that love and have their life totally changed.

~~~

Personality is not how you manifest in the
world. It is how you react to the world.
Change your reaction, change your world.

We all drink from the same river because
we are that river; it moves and flows
through each and every one of us.
Let's be mindful not to contaminate it.

~~~

If you allow yourself to be in
a state of knowing absolutely nothing,
you just might glimpse what actually Is.

The only reason we feel held back,
or stuck in our lives, is because we are
unable to let go of something
that is preventing our forward movement.

~~~

Be yourself until there is no self to be.

If you look carefully you will see that
life actually stands still, vibrating with
immense passion as it quietly waits for you
to jump in and partake of its essence.

∼∼∼

Everything that went before
was in preparation for this moment.

PART TWO

Facing the fear

It had gone on for so long, this constant constriction in my solar plexus that I had identified as fear. I was exhausted by its hold on me and yet what was I to do? On this particular day I decided that I was going to be done with it—no longer would I allow this thing called fear to dictate my life. No matter what, it had to end.

I went into my bedroom and lay on the bed. I could feel this familiar feeling rising up in my chest and into the very heart of my being. But instead of resisting, I simply spoke to it. "Here I am. You can have me. Take me and do with me what you wish. I will not resist or fight you. You are allowed and I welcome you." As I lay on the bed I waited and watched. I watched as this thing called fear, this intense energy that had for so long been my enemy, became stronger and stronger within my body. I felt it entering from the right of my solar plexus and move toward the center of my chest. It gathered strength as it moved. I did nothing but allow. It reached a crescendo in the center of my solar plexus;

so powerful was its strength, that I felt I was finished. This energy called fear consumed me so fully, and still I allowed and watched.

As it entered into my heart, I felt myself break. There was an audible crash and I knew this was the actual end, the end of me. I saw a cross in my solar plexus and in that resounding crash I saw it break and split. I had surrendered to this force so completely and now I was gone. And, in that moment of complete acceptance of this thing called fear that I had for so long fought and resisted, it retreated. It began to move from my heart and sideways along and to the left side of my body until I could no longer feel it.

In the facing of this thing called fear, I had learned to trust, allow and surrender. There is another lesson here and it is: Fear of fear only gives more fear, so whatever you do, never treat fear with fear.

Speak your Truth where your Truth wants to be heard; Truth then will magnify itself in front of your very eyes and miracles will happen.
Truth is universal and belongs to all.

～～

Get in touch with yourself, and whatever wants to get in touch with you will.

Freedom from suffering comes as a direct result
of your ability to self-observe without reacting.

~~~

Whenever you see a body, a physical body,
that you might have a judgement of,
ask yourself: What lesson is that person having
to master through that body? From that inquiry
true compassion has the capacity to be born.

Life will go on regardless, so why not
release your hold on the reins?

~~~

The moment you have a personal investment in
the teacher, he ceases to be able to teach you.

Can you listen without a sense of self?
To do this is to listen with compassion.
To truly listen is an act of Love.

~~~

In this moment you can decide
to let everyone off the hook. When you do this
you also let yourself off the hook.

True commitment is not a prison; it's a freedom.

～～

Consciousness lives outside of the brain
and the body. The body does not make
consciousness, consciousness makes the body.
Therefore there is no death, just the withdrawal
of the consciousness from the body.

Wherever there is division there is insensitivity.
Sensitivity cannot live with division.

~~~

Do not form any opinions or draw
any conclusions about yourself or another.
When we do this we inhibit and frame life
and set up a barrier to true relationship.

To be in a state of non-reactive awareness to life
is to be in a state of living—truly alive.

～～～

You'll never have to give anything up if you
allow things to leave you.

You cannot change what you are
by pretending to not be it.

~~~

Enlightenment is a sensation of your self
as nothing, when all the edges roll away
and there is nothing.

The length of time you take to act on what you see will determine the depth of the suffering that you have to suffer.

~~~

Make all of life's decisions without fear of loss or hope for gain.

When you choose to be in health let it mean
health to yourself and to all around you.
To be in health should not be a self-centered
action; rather it should include every single
relationship you are having, have had
or ever will have.

～

What could be so important that
you have to be right?

Choose to be less a container of the conditioned mind and more a vehicle for Love.

~~~

Relationship exists without friendship but friendship cannot exist without relationship.

Silence exists where the self is not.
This silence is the silence of no inner movement
or reaction at all.

～～

You don't need to know; you just think you do.

You are what you are, to be what you are,
not to deny what you are.

～～

You cannot frame the un-frameable.
Life is un-frameable, so do not try to frame it.
Live without edges.

Being is personal; non-being is impersonal and at one with Divinity, the cosmic light projector.

~~~

In life you get exactly what you allow yourself to be given.

People are not relating; images are.

~~~

Never try to gain brownie points
at someone else's expense.

There is nothing other than this moment.
What you think and entertain in this moment
is what your life will be.

∿

You are judged only as much as you need
to be judged in order that you may stop judging.

You are a manifestation of the mind of God.

~~~

All I know is I don't know what I don't know.

When it comes to relationship with our
fellow neighbor, seek the common ground.
Intelligence seeks the common ground;
ignorance seeks the difference.

~~~

You cannot know anyone
because no one is fixed.

Decision disallows procrastination;
procrastination disallows life.
Be in decision and be in life.

～～

The level to which you judge yourself is the
level to which you judge others. When self-
judgement ends, judgement of others also ends.

Absolute self-honesty
is the secret to inner change.

~~~

Have no expectation of people
and they will delight you.

When you listen, listen to the interval between
the words and hear what is actually being said.
Never listen to the words alone but also to the
place from which they are spoken.
This is the true art of listening.

~~~

If the shoe doesn't fit, why keep trying to
squeeze your foot into it?

Do not live life backwards.

～～

Resistance is caused by the notion
that life is fixed when it definitely is not.

At the center of every human being is a core of benevolence. Always give others the opportunity to be benevolent.

～～～

Life should not be about: "I did something wrong in the past." Rather, ask yourself: "What am I doing in the present?"

It is a fact: There is nothing other than this.
Live with that knowledge and allow everything
that is not of this, to drop from you.

~~~

No matter what you are feeling or what comes
your way in this life, cultivate an attitude of
gratitude. There is nothing without gratitude.

You see society the way you perceive it to be.
Change your perception, change society.

~~~

You manifest your life in each and
every moment. All that is your life is a
manifestation of you. You are the magician.

You cannot have a button pushed if there isn't
already a button within you to be pushed.
The button belongs to you. Do not make
others responsible for your reactions.

~~~

You are the author of your own story.
Are you writing that story as you live
or is the story already written?

Your thoughts, feelings, and standards
are your life guides. Let others have theirs.
End the judgement.

～～～

The temptation is to believe what the world
tells you when, in fact, there is no power or
reality in its lies. The power lies only in what
you attach to the world beliefs in your thought.
Do not believe this world, rather find out
for yourself if what the world tells you
is true or not. Here in lies a major key to the
coming into the sensation of Truth—Reality.

Truth lies between the belief in good and evil.

~~~

The body is not Life; Life is the body.

The only way you can get to the truth about
what you are feeling is to tell, at least to
yourself, the truth about what you feel.

~~~

There is nothing other than This.
When you truly see that there is nothing
other than This, then you become totally
responsible for yourself and all around you,
no matter what course your life takes or how
you choose to live it. You also begin the process
of creating what your This, Is.

Power is neutral;
it's what we do with it that isn't.

~~~

There is a saying "What doesn't kill you makes
you stronger." But in fact it should kill you.
It should kill the small self which is only
interested in me, me, me, I, I, I, so that
the big Self, the true Self, which is the
Divine spark within each of us, can truly
be born and begin to live your life.

When you cultivate an attitude of gratitude
no matter what comes your way, you transcend
the world of opposites, which is this world,
and begin to live from the world of Truth,
which just Is.

~~~

Calling an emotion negative causes a greater
resistance to it and a stronger desire to get
rid of it, thus strengthening it and giving it
more power. Let go of the idea of good or bad
emotions and allow yourself to feel.

Instead of thinking: "What can I get out of life?"
Why not think: "What can I give?"

~~~

If you cannot approach your fellow
human beings with an attitude of goodwill,
then it might be better to leave yourself
at home alone until you can.

Rid yourself of all expectation and
allow what Is, to reveal Itself.

~~~

Whenever we think of ourselves as being
anything, we fall short of being able to be.
Have no idea of yourself and discover freedom.

Why am I so arrogant as to think that I have to forgive someone? Who am I to forgive you, who am I to judge you? The idea that I have to forgive you, is learned. When we see that there is nothing and no one to forgive, then maybe we are a little closer to the ending of the self and the birth of the YOU.

～～～

Relationships always mirror to us our internal state. If we are wise we will take note of this and address ourselves accordingly, and without any judgement of the mirror.

You have already survived what you are afraid
of feeling, and it didn't kill you the first time,
so it won't kill you now.

PART THREE

To be nothing

The heat was blistering that day and the silence was everywhere. I was walking across the Outback on land where possibly no human had ever walked, a land uncontaminated by thought and the meanderings of a million minds. The feeling of emptiness was tangible. It was as if I had entered a library with no books, the shelves empty and free of thought. I could hear the land's silence, and my mind settled in this stillness of no thought.

Then I heard words coming to me from deep within: "To live in the noise of the mind is to be in the dream. You must wake from the dream to experience peace and freedom. If you could drop every idea and belief that you have of yourself, you will come upon your essence. Here is the substance of your being and your union with the source. To be nothing is to be the absolute heartbeat of everything."

The words were a challenge to me: Could I exist without the noise? Could I put down all that I had accumulated in this life? Was I prepared to discard all concerns of the mind with its projections of past and future? Was it possible to end all belief in myself? Was I prepared to put it all to one side? How could I live here in this new way?

These questions seemed to answer themselves in a simple yet profound revelation. Behind all the garments of belief, desire, and my sense of self, there is a ground and substance. It is an inner space within me. If I pay attention to it instead of my mind, if I simply trust this space and silence, if I stay out of the way long enough—it will live me. And in that living, it will allow the real me, the free, innocent and uncluttered me to be born.

I felt an immense gratitude for the lesson this dry arid place had given me and I felt a duty to leave it untouched by any residue of me.

Our need for a reputation is a block to our
authenticity and inner freedom. As long as you
desire anyone to think or not think anything
about you, you cannot be authentic and free.

~~~

The ending of identification with anything
is freedom.

It is the light of truth that burns out
the illusion of despair.

~~~

The beliefs that you hold about yourself, or
indeed anyone or anything, are only as strong
as the strength of your attachment to them and
the level at which you have personalized them.

After insight, comes action. Action will only come about through discipline. Discipline allows you to grow from insight and is the tool you must use to enable this growth. There can be no growth without self-discipline.

~~~

Love is actually chasing us. If only we would stop for a moment and sense it.
Ah the wonder of Life!

Truth lives in the Silence. This is not the Silence that occurs when the things of this world are quiet, rather it is a state of inner Silence that is revealed when thought of any kind has ended. This happens when we are able to look at the world, both inner and outer, without making any assessment of what it is that we are seeing and without an iota of belief in good and bad, right and wrong, pleasure or pain.

There are no profound states;
there are only states we don't yet know.

~~~

Belief begins with the primary belief which is
the belief in two powers: the power of good and
the power of bad. In order to come upon Truth,
which just Is, you have to end your belief
in either of these, and that means the good
as well as the bad.

It is better to be in the dark to your self
than not acting on what you see.

~~~

Life usually begins as a selfish program but only
in order for it to take you to a selfless place.

Can you look at any person, place,
or thing, without an inner assessor making an
assessment? Try it and see what happens.

~~~

When you are walking in the right direction,
everything that you need to enable you to keep
on walking is freely, openly, and
effortlessly given.

Power comes in the knowledge
of your powerlessness.

~~~

Belief: I haven't got enough.
Reality: I have more than I need.
Which state are you in?

It would seem that many times in this world we
are like children in a sweet shop who want all of
the sweets but can't handle the sugar hit.
If that is the case, then it might be advisable to
be more discerning in, not only the choice,
but also the amount of sweets that we choose.

~~~

You never arrive.
You are always at the beginning.

Life isn't about holding on to things. It's about allowing everything to pass. All things must die so that Life can live. We hold on for dear life never realizing that the holding on is our very death. We are our own executioner.

～～～

You are the editor of your own life.

Fear only becomes fear when you
believe in it, name it, run from it, and
create a division between yourself and it.

～～～

Fear and dislike of being judged, almost always
arise from a place of judgement, dislike,
and non-acceptance of yourself.

How can I sit with you
if I cannot sit with myself?

~~~

Within each one of us lives an utterly
silent state that knows nothing of the things of
this world, and holds no belief in good and bad,
pleasure and pain, right and wrong.

In order to have the revelation of Reality, it
is essential that you allow yourself to think
outside of the box and to consider that what
you give importance and power to, what you
think and believe, just might not be true,
or indeed, have any substance at all
other than what you have given to it.

~~~

You are only as acceptable to others
as you are to yourself.

Get out of your head and into your heart.

~~~

Take a moment to realize that the actions
of a person are not necessarily the who of
the person, meaning a person is not necessarily
his actions. It would then follow that just
because you may or may not condone a person's
actions, does not mean that you have to judge,
condemn, or even praise him.

You are here to be what you are,
not to deny what you are.

~~~

Intention is the seed of Life.
What is your life's intention?

The way in which you relate to others will dictate the type of relationships that you have.

～～～

Consider the possibility that every human being is fundamentally good and wants more than anything to do good, and see how your life changes.

Love isn't divisible; Love just Is.

~~~

At what level does your mind interpret
that which it becomes aware of? At the
material level, which is the world of opposites,
or at the spiritual level, which just Is?

Give yourself permission to do what makes your Soul sing, and, if you don't already know what that is, then find out.

~~~

It is important to remember that when you meet someone, anyone, you meet their entire history right up to and including this moment—and maybe even into the future. You do not know the details and events, but you do know what it is to be human. With that in mind always meet a person with compassion.

If you have to hang on to anything
then it doesn't really belong to you.

～～

Resistance only has the power
that you give to it in your resistance.

This life isn't meant to be about being a clone of
other people in any way, shape, or form;
it's about being you, and not in a reactive way,
but just because that is what you are here to be.

~~~

Judgement underlies suffering.

Be open to learning the lesson
of a person's reaction to you.

~~~

Belief is the block to the knowledge of what Is.

The missing link is self-discipline.
Self-discipline can often mean practicing
things that aren't normal for you to do
or not do, and not practicing things that are
normal for you to do or not do, until they
become normal and natural.

～～

You cannot get where you think you are going
without leaving where you think you are.

There is an inner state of allowing
with no idea of doing or non-doing.

~~~

The most important thing there is to learn in
life is equanimity. That means to be able to
sit with what Is, both internal and external,
without reacting to it. However, this state of
being, in no way inhibits or denies action in
your life, rather it promotes an action that is
devoid of reaction and just Is.

Anything that I think I am has come about
through an investment in a belief of this world.
What I actually Am, has nothing to do
with this world.

～～

Can you look at fear without being afraid of
fear (which is the past), but just look at fear?

Do not think it noble to deny
what you are feeling, rather realize
it is noble to feel without reaction.

~~~

All the words mean nothing without action;
they mean absolutely nothing.

Truth is something you live,
not something you know.

Never negate or dismiss your longing.
It is a gift and an end in itself. It is its own
answer to all of your questions.

We hold something in common with every
person we meet, hard as it may be to see
at times, this is a fact. With that in mind,
don't judge others—just receive them.

~~~

The question is: What is the Silence?
The posing of that question is
the hearing of the Silence.

In relationship, rather than thinking in terms
of being taken from, why not think in terms
of wanting to give?

~~~

Admitting where you need to change is
one thing; acting on that knowledge is another.

The illusion of this world is not in
what we think we see outside of ourselves;
rather it is within us that the illusion exists.
It is in our senses. Our senses lie to us all of
the time in relation to our perception of what
appears to be outside of us.

~~~

To be aware is one thing; but the way
in which your mind interprets that awareness
is another and dictates the level of your
perception and consciousness.

Our thoughts and beliefs create our reality
and then we hang on to that for dear life
and identify with it. But this creation has
no substance and can crash at any time.

~~~

True sensitivity comes when you realize that
every person you meet, regardless of your
opinion of him or your reaction to him, should
always be treated with humanity. Always treat
your fellow human beings with humanity.

Is your attitude to life "I haven't got enough,"
or have you reached the realization that
you have more than you need?

~~~

Material reality is the belief in two powers,
good and bad. Spiritual reality is
the perception of what Is.

Can you live your life without concern
for what others think about you, and not in a
reactionary way, yet still maintain sensitivity
to your fellow human beings?

～～～

There is no me in humility.
Humility is where you are not.

In matters of Truth, Truth will only reveal Itself
to you if It is desired for Its own sake and not
for any other. By this is meant, that Truth
has to be desired always and only
for the sake of Truth.

≈≈≈

Always be in a state of decision.
Decision pinpoints life yet allows it to
expand eternally from that point. Decision
magnifies your life and is totally natural.

Mental freedom occurs as you stop identifying
yourself with the content of the mind.

～～

Your life is shaped by the thoughts you think.

Once the desire for a reputation ends,
with it also go many of the beliefs that you
hold about yourself, which are all lies anyway.

~~~

The illusion has been invented by belief.
All belief is the essence and continuation
of illusion.

The question isn't whether or not there is
a God, a something behind what we call life;
nor is it a question of that something getting in
touch with me. Rather let the question be:
"Am I willing to give up the human condition
which believes in two powers, good and evil, to
find out if there is one original cause,
one power, a Divine presence, behind what we
call life?" And if there is; where does that exist?

People, places, and things are transient.
Don't make them fixed.

～～～

When you have no idea of yourself, see how
eventually the world has no idea of you as well;
and even if it does, it cannot touch you.
Ah, how sweet it is. Here in lies the freedom.

PART FOUR

Sitting in stillness

Sitting in stillness, and here we are talking about inner stillness, cannot occur unless the individual has first begun to sit. And what is meant by "sitting"? Well, it is simply to make a decision to sit alone (with no activity or distractions) with oneself for a period of time on a daily basis. When we do this, we give ourselves the opportunity to see the inner terrain of the mind, the me that we think we are, and at the same time we are also given the ability to see its hold on us and how we react to these mental images, thoughts, ideas, and feelings.

If practiced long enough, we become free of the desire to be involved in the demands of the mind, other than to see and watch and wait. Now we find ourselves in a simple state of allowing, with neither reaction nor resistance, and without any attachment to the picture that the mind is presenting upon the screen of our life. At this point we realize that we can choose to focus our attention somewhere else, we can begin to sense something new that exists beyond the mind. We are now less a victim of the mind, more able to be clear and direct in just where we want to focus our attention.

When we have achieved a consistent practice of sitting, the cleansing of the mind occurs. We find that we are able to sit with ourselves with no reaction at all to what is going on. As we continue to practice sitting in this way, just sitting here with whatever shows up, there is the possibility of us ending any interest in the things of the mind. It is then that we can come upon an inner stillness and silence that is so enticing in its perfume, that our preference for it far outweighs our attachment to the meanderings of the mind.

It is now that we see that there is a domain, a field of existence, beyond the mind. In this insight we have the opportunity to remain within the silence and stillness of this field with no thought or attachment to the mind. We can see beyond the boundary, the boundary that is the self with which we have identified, the self we believe our self to be. We are now beyond the boundary. We find we are immersed in a silence so loud that it drowns out the noise of this world and the noise of the identified self. It is then that you can finally sit in this stillness and partake of its divine silence and love.

The greatest fear is the fear of the annihilation
of the self. The fact is that in order to come
upon truth and reality, the self has to be
annihilated, so that the true essence,
the Divine spark, can be fully realized.

~~~

Truth exists in the vacuum that is revealed
when you give up the belief in good and evil.

The level of consciousness that you live from
determines your mind's interpretation
of what it sees.

~~~

Do not hold any thoughts, opinions, judgement,
ideas or beliefs about yourself; they serve only
to diminish what you actually are. The truth
is that you are much, much, much more than
what you think you are.

Your life is already all around you:
What do you chose to pick from it?

~~~

There is nothing outside of yourself.

Ponder this: Have you ever asked yourself
"Where do I exist in the body?"
And, if you have, did you get an answer?

~~~

Allow yourself to be in discovery without
any idea of what you will discover in all areas
of your life. Discovery, without the burden of
the past, which means without any idea of itself,
is new and innocent and free of fear.

There is only one teacher and it lies within
the depths and silence of your Soul.
It is to That that you must ultimately refer;
all the rest is the playground, always and only
to be used as a stepping stone to It.

～

There is nothing that you are not.

All that I am is all that you are, and all that that is, is Love. There is only one obligation in life and that is to Love.

~~~

It's what you do with what you feel that counts, not what you feel. When you know this truth, you are no longer a victim of your feelings and there is no need to deny or repress anything that comes up.

Don't be afraid if you hit a brick wall
inside of yourself; there is no reason
to bring anything in—just stay there.

~~~

You are the heartbeat
in the consciousness of God.

Love isn't about feeling that you love someone;
it's about others feeling love from you.

~~~

Poverty exists because we believe in it,
when in fact, all that exists
is endless abundance.

The world is a provision.

~~~

There is only one mind, the Divine mind.
So, what is the human mind?
The human mind is the conditioned aspect
of the Divine mind. When you end the
conditioning you find yourself
within the heart of the Divine.

We have taken words and made them our
reality without even being truly aware
of what we are saying.

~~~

In this world we are visitors.
With that in mind, rather than thinking
"What can I get while I am here?", why not
consider "What will I leave when I depart?"

The action of Truth within the individual
is the only power that changes him.

〜〜〜

It is one thing to be sensitive and quite another
to be an outpouring of sensitivity.
All too often our sensitivity is only
towards ourselves, when of course that is not
what it is for at all; rather it is for us to be
sensitive to all around us, and even including
ourselves, but not as a contraction inward,
more as an expansion outward.

Immortality is a state of consciousness
that is accessible by all, which, when sensed,
has no concern whether or not it is
translated to the body.

～～～

Belief only has the power that you give to it
in your belief in it.

The only real sensation is that of Love.
All else is but a temptation to make us believe
in a power other than Love.

~~~

The only effort required in life
is the effort to be conscious.

You die because you never lived.

～～～

Two very important questions to ponder:
Why am I here? What is my passion?

Life isn't meant to be a series of problems.
It's simply a sequence of events and
circumstances in the form of people, places,
and things to be faced with less reaction
and more love.

～～～

Interpretation is a barrier to Truth.

Nothing belongs to you; you just think it does.

~~~

The most powerful beliefs are the ones
we hold about ourselves, which, in turn,
dictate the way in which we want others to
think about us. When you break these beliefs
you set yourself free.

You end up exactly where you are meant to be.

~~~

Let the silence roar so loudly
that it drowns out the noise of this world.

Suffering is your future state calling you to give birth to it. It is your Soul calling to be born.

～～～

There is an internal state to be attained where, what looks like an error, a fault, a good or a bad, is no longer seen as such—but even before that, when it is seen, it is given no power at all.

If you give up the world, the world will give up you and Reality will step in. But what is the world as we know it? Is it not the conditioned mind which is made up of all sorts of beliefs and superstitions? It might be worth looking within and questioning, to see if in fact, any of what the mind believes, is actually true at all.

~~~

You are the final piece of perfection married to all the other pieces of perfection in this great and wondrous tapestry that we call Life.

All that I am is consciousness and the level of consciousness that is revealed within me will determine my perception of the world.

～～～

The only things we know
are what we don't know.

The only way to the Soul is to feel.

~~~

Everything that exists within the human mind
is learned. The true nature of the mind
is innocent and uncluttered. In that state
the mind is silent and free.

Wherever you go, wherever you are,
be it here, there, or anywhere, remember this:
The perfume of your presence remains.

～～～

The desire for self-knowledge based on
self-interest is the very thing which prevents
Self-knowing, which is true compassion.

God wants to fulfill Itself through you, but you
want to fulfill yourself through the world.
As long as you are seeking fulfillment
through the world, there can be no peace
and no lasting and permanent realization
of the presence of God.

~~~

Life keeps throwing the same thing at you
until you do it right.

Every person, place, or thing that comes to you
will be met at the level from where you live.
In short, you will meet everything
from where you are at.

~~~

Live with Intention;
Intention and its action are not separate.

The level of your consciousness determines
the way in which your mind perceives.
Change your consciousness, change your mind.

~~~

I do not have to understand to accept;
rather I have to accept to understand. Let it be.

Learn to say "I don't know." It is a wonderful
place to be where freedom is often found.

~~~

The ego, meaning the small me,
only invests itself in the mundane.

Truth lies in the silence
of the interval between the words.

~~~

If you know that black is black, why would you
entertain red as black? Trust yourself.

When it comes to good, in this world good is
the opposite of bad. But, in reality, which has no
knowledge or sensation of opposites,
Good is All and All is Good. In other words:
Good just Is. Establish a consciousness of Good.

～～～

The world that you behold arises
from an inner state within yourself.

Life is not meant to be a project on fear.

~~~

In this world we are antennae; antennae to this world, which is the world of beliefs and opposites, and antennae to the Divine, which is the world of Truth and Reality. In which direction is your antenna aimed?

True understanding comes when we
can understand without using the mind.
Understanding without the mind
is pure knowing.

~~~

The only reason sickness looks like sickness
is because that is what we believe it to be.

Knowing comes from the great Unknown.

~~~

God is where I am not.

Everything exists within you.

~~~

Life is a journey in the present moment without
a past or a future. Allow life to be just that.

Give to others the Light that is being given
to you. It's not yours to keep so pass it on.

~~~

Truth lies outside of the herd. But you can still
be in the herd and live from Truth;
you don't need to isolate.

True living is a non-reactive state. To be truly
alive is to be totally non-reactive to anything:
person, place, thought, or thing. Only then
is a person free of fear.

~~~

Pride is the false ego telling you
that you achieved something on your own.

Pure consciousness is the substance,
source, law, and cause of all creation;
therefore what consciousness is, is what I am.
"I Am" is what consciousness Is.

~~~

The emptying of the self is the allowing
of what Is to be born.

The only disease is in the going against
of our nature. The only disease is due to
resistance to our true nature. Our true nature is
always innocent, pure, benevolent, and loving.

≈≈≈

You are the book of Life.

PART FIVE

The boundary

You are the boundary; the "you" with all its be-lief and identification; the "you" that you think yourself to be. But once you drop all of that, once you allow all the edges of the boundary to dis-solve and melt away, you find yourself in an end-less sea of perfection and love.

Beyond the boundary, there is a dimension of living, a field of existence untouched by human thought. This field is the very source of human existence and indeed it is our birthright to re-member, know, and sense this field. In order to touch and remain in this unconditioned state of love and innocence, the individual has to sur-render the boundary and dive deep into the sea of truth and love. In that surrender is freedom and peace, and the unquestionable knowledge of what is actually real and what is definitely not.

Now you are beyond the boundary, this life can be truly lived, free of all image and idea. Each wisdom gives you the opportunity to come to that silence, to be still. In short to be "Beyond the Boundary".

Each and every one of us is a mirror
to the internal state of each and every one of us.

~~~

Right action has no motive. It just is.

Where there is no self, there is no problem.

∼∼∼

You will see me as you perceive me to be
not as I actually am. If you can see me as
I actually am, then you will not be concerned
with how you perceive me, or indeed even
have any perception of me.

Do not resist the resistance.

～

You become what you think you are.
You are what you perceive yourself to be.

When you reach the state of having no idea
of yourself, there is an opportunity to
discover what you actually are.

～～～

All that you want, you already have,
and all that you have, you don't need to want.

The sum of your life, both internal
and external, up to and including this moment,
is a manifestation of the decisions and choices
that you have made. Take responsibility.

~~~

The mirror that you provide for me is only
to reflect back my inability to love you
without conditions.

Destiny is not fixed.

~~~

Allow Life to express itself as you
rather than trying to express yourself as Life.

Life is in abundance and in abundance I live.

～～～

Choose to be present.

Power lives in the realization
that there is no power.

~~~

If I am not able to come to you with a sense of
goodwill, then I will not come to you at all.

It is only by knowing what Love isn't
that we can know what Love is.

~~~

You are your own pharmacy and you can access
any state within your self.

The world is nothing other than what you
believe it to be. End all belief and
see the nothingness of this world.
Therein is your freedom.

～～～

Whatever you think I am has nothing to do
with what I actually am.

Surrender is the key to change; and there is
only one type of surrender. It happens in the
moment when we fully, freely, and openly see
that I cannot do this; I have no power to do this.
I cannot change myself. In that moment
we are at a point where the hand of God can
rise up from within us and do whatever it is
that needs to be done. This could come in the
form of a spontaneous happening or a slow and
ongoing one; but be assured, it does come.

Can you look at any person, place, or thing,
either outside of yourself or within,
without forming any idea of what it is
that you are looking at? It can be done;
but it requires immense effort, energy,
and a discipline which is Love, and needs
to be attempted without any thought of gain
or reward, but just because it has to be done.

~~~

When we are speaking, develop the ability
to be aware of the place from where we speak.
In that way, we can choose carefully and with
seriousness, whether or not we should speak
at all, until we suddenly realize that we are not
speaking any more, rather we are being spoken.

The small I, is the aspect of myself that desires to be thought of as something by both myself and others. Can I live without any need for that?

～

You don't need to know; you just think you do.

What we believe about others and ourselves, is not true. Belief is not true. Anything that is here today but gone tomorrow, anything that is true today but a lie tomorrow, in fact, anything that is able to change and is not fixed and permanent, is not true. Wouldn't it then be fair to say, that all of our beliefs lie in one or all of these categories? Belief is not true.

~~~

Life, death, and immortality, all phase in and out of each other and are not separate in any way.

That which Is, is that which I Am.

~~~

Freedom comes through
freedom from the self—yourself.

There is a space within each one of us
where nothing Is.

~~~

Thought stops when there is no me—no person
making an assessment.

Live life in the moment, acting on those moments as you create your future. Acting in the moment is the creation of your future.

~~~

Consciousness is all that I am, and all that Is, is Consciousness.

Silence lives in the present.

~~~

We all have the possibility of becoming so
highly evolved in consciousness that all
you see in me and all I see in you is Love.

This world—meaning the level of
consciousness within the individual that
believes in two powers, the power of good and
the power of bad—is at best, a world full of
opportunities to deny and look through those
beliefs, and hence come upon Truth, or,
at worst, a total distraction from Truth.
Where do you stand?

~~~

Is your perception of the world
based on belief or Reality?

There is only Here. Here being the only place
that there is; there is nowhere else. The only
thing that changes is the level of consciousness
from which you perceive Here, but you always
are, always were and always will be—Here.
There is nowhere else, absolutely nowhere else,
to either go or be. All states of perception
are within you and that also includes your
perception of Here. But you are
and always will be ... Here.

When you make a decision, the action that
follows should keep reinforcing the decision.
Therein lies the work.

~~~

The sensation of Truth, God, the Is,
exists in the vacuum that is revealed
when we give up the belief in two powers,
the power of evil as well as the power of good.

In order to know Truth, you have to be prepared to empty yourself of yourself. This is what is meant by dying daily.

～

When the trying to get ends, you are getting a little closer to Truth.

There is no transition from Here to
another place. The only transition is in the way
in which your consciousness perceives Here.

~~~

You cannot be where you aren't already;
you can only be where you are.

All you have is this moment, and it is here
that you can address and deal with whatever
is showing up. If you live this way, then there is
no need to relate to or think of the past,
or indeed the future.

~~~

Let your heart dictate and your head will follow.

Truth has no concern for the comforts
and desires of this world.

~~~

Everything exists within the vacuum
of the unconditioned mind.

Life is a movement; move with It.

~~~

The only true state is the state of revelation.
Revelation is the only reality.

Wisdom is there for the taking
if you allow yourself to receive It.

～

Where there is a shred of attachment,
there is no Love.

Now hear this because it is deeply important:
You cannot sense Infinity from the finite senses.
To be able to do so would be a contradiction
in terms. In order to sense Infinity you have
to develop a higher sense, a sense that has no
attachment to the desires of this world. In fact,
this new sense already exists within you, but
the subtlety of its nature makes it impossible
to sense through the noise and distractions
of this world. Instead, it waits silently for you
to be still enough for it to make Itself known.
Once sensed, it is your doorway to Reality,
Immortality, and the ever expanding knowledge
of Truth. It is your Soul, give birth to her.

Observation of a person is one thing,
judgement is another. Can you observe
without judgement?

~~~

Nothing can be seen correctly
when viewed through the lens of belief.

Because I think I am a human being, I am
governed by the thoughts, feelings, and beliefs
of this world. But in fact, my true nature is not
that of a human being. My true and original
nature is Divine. I am a spark of the Divine,
a beat in the heart of God. But in order to see
the reality of this truth, I need to give up any
investment or belief in myself as only human.

~~~

The emptying of the self
is the gateway to Truth.

What you believe is what you will perceive.

~~~

It is my false concept of Life
that needs adjusting, not Life itself.

There are changing states of consciousness,
but there is no other place than Here.

～～～

The veil that separates you from Reality
is the veil of belief. Draw back the veil of belief
and see yourself as you actually are
and Life as it actually is.

Change does not exist in Truth.

~~~

Whoever told you that the individual ultimately
develops to such a high state of consciousness
that he finally merges with a blob of oneness?
It is a lie. You go on forever in an expanding
conscious awareness of your particular aspect
of Reality which includes the sensation of One.

The outer is born of the inner.
Our outer conditions are born
of our inner state of consciousness.

～～

You are not a who, you are a what.
So the question is: What am I?

Explore the possibility of seeing what you don't yet know about your self instead of always focusing on what you do know or what you think you know. What you don't know you don't know about yourself, is just sitting there waiting for you to see and has immense importance.

The moment you see through the illusion of belief, you are free. This is an ongoing process as every belief, both conscious and unconscious, has to be seen through and dropped, as and when it appears.

Can you sit in the face and presence
of what is without reacting? Try it.

~~~

Life is meant to be lived without any idea
of getting, or indeed, losing anything.

When I think that I know you, then what I am
actually doing is framing and limiting you
and this means that I do not love you.
Love has no idea of the thing that it loves.
It does not make a person limited or fixed
and it doesn't allow me to have a fixed idea
or knowledge of you. To say that I know you,
is to have framed and fixed you in my mind.
This in turn is not love and actually means
that I do not love you. Love has no idea
of the thing that it loves.

Not believing in something is the same
as believing. In other words, believing and
not believing are one and the same thing.
In fact, often, not believing requires a lot
more energy and resolve. But, in order to truly
discover, you need to be totally open. Let go of
the need to believe or to not believe and allow
yourself the discovery of all that Is.

〜〜〜

All that you are is a vehicle for consciousness.
You are here because pure consciousness
wants to be seen in all Its glory.

Spirituality is the knowledge of IS.

~~~

Creation is in a state of experience and
you are that. You are the experience of Creation.

Do not invest in believing
that your nature is a particular way.

～～～

Experience your own in-side-ness
and never again feel like an outsider. That is
the key to your sense of connection to all of Life,
from the beginning and on into eternity.

There is only one Truth; but there are endless
variations, sensations, and perceptions of
that Truth, as it exposes itself within the
consciousness of the individual.

〜〜〜

You cannot be yourself
until there is no self to be.

May the heartache of yesterday
give birth to the joy of today.

Your Wisdoms

~~~

~~~

A LITTLE BOOK OF WISDOMS

~~~

~~~

~~~

A LITTLE BOOK OF WISDOMS

~~~

Made in the USA
Monee, IL
03 August 2020

37504566R00127